Stress-Free Security

OrangeBooks Publication

1st Floor, Rajhans Arcade, Mall Road, Kohka, Bhilai, Chhattisgarh 490020

Website: **www.orangebooks.in**

First Edition, 2025

ISBN: 978-93-6554-360-5

Price: Rs. 333.00

Printed in India

STRESS-FREE SECURITY

A YOGIC PATH TO HOLISTIC SECURITY—FOR FAMILIES, ORGANIZATIONS, BUSINESSES, AND NATIONS

JITENDRA NATH PALEM

OrangeBooks Publication
www.orangebooks.in

Preface

In a world filled with passwords, locks, cameras, Pin numbers and codes, we find ourselves more anxious than ever. Even with all the progress in technology and security, fear still follows us—around our homes, inside our systems, and deep within our minds. What are we really protecting if our hearts are still restless?

This book was born from a simple truth: real security is not just about walls, weapons, or software. It begins within—a calm mind, a steady heart, and a peaceful way of living. The ancient wisdom of yoga teaches us that peace is the strongest shield, and awareness is the best kind of protection.

But let's be clear—staying calm doesn't mean we ignore danger. It doesn't mean we quietly accept harm. A yogic mindset is not about being weak. It's about being alert, strong, and wise.

We live in a world where attacks can happen, where some people lose their way and do harm to others. A peaceful mind helps us see danger clearly. A steady heart helps us think before we act. A strong body moves with purpose, not panic. When we are calm inside, we can protect better on the outside.

it means being deeply aware, prepared, and wise. A calm mind sees danger clearly. A centred heart makes decisions without panic. A resilient body acts swiftly and effectively.

When we cultivate inner stability, we don't become passive—we become powerful. We respond instead of react. We act with both strength and compassion. We train better, lead better, and protect better—whether in a battlefield, a home, or a server room

We will also explore why some people lose their common sense and turn to harmful behaviour. Often, it comes from stress, fear, or emotional pain. This book will offer ways to prevent such changes—through ethical training, clear thinking, emotional support, and a sense of inner connection. These are not just spiritual ideas—they are practical tools for building a safer world.

"Stress-Free Security" is not just a dream. It is a way of living. And like all meaningful paths, it starts from within and flows outward into action.

To those who have purchased this book, thank you—from the bottom of my heart. Your interest in this journey shows that you care not just about safety, but also about peace. I hope the pages ahead give you strength, insight, and a deep sense of calm.

Whether you're a Policy maker, Business man, security expert, a soldier, a parent, or simply someone looking for peace in a noisy world—this book is for you. May it help you see that true safety comes when strength and stillness come together

Acknowledgement

I am deeply grateful to each and every one of you who has chosen to embark on this journey with me. Your purchase of this book is a testament to your desire for a holistic approach to security—a quest to safeguard not only your career and finances but also the well-being of your loved ones.

Whether you're a technologist, manager, leader, commander, Major, administrator, student, CEO, CISO, business professional, homemaker, academician, teacher, or simply an individual curious about security best practices (Physical, digital, Cyber information, data), this book is designed to empower you and your organization. The insights shared within its pages are not merely the product of my own experiences, but rather a synthesis of ancient Yogic wisdom and modern security practices.

My journey into the world of Yoga began over a decade ago through self-practice, driven by a personal quest for balance and well-being. However, a significant turning point came when my manager, Mr. Sivaprakash Palaniswamy—a seasoned IT professional(Vice President in IT Industry) —introduced me to the field of Yoga Therapy. His thoughtful recommendation, made in response to my health concerns, opened a new dimension of Yoga that led to a profound transformation in my life, extending far beyond physical wellness into mental clarity, emotional resilience, and spiritual growth. I extend my heartfelt gratitude to him, whose thoughtful guidance became the catalyst for a transformative journey into the deeper realms of Yoga

As a Director in the Global IT Industry specialized in Quality and Data Science Domain and a dedicated practitioner of Yoga for over a decade, I am honoured to share the profound insights that have shaped my journey. My long-standing practice—deeply enriched by the reverential study of sacred scriptures such as the Shrimad Bhagavad Gita, Yoga Vasistham, Shrimad Ramayana, Sri Guru Charitra, the noble path of Ashtanga Yoga, and classical Ayurvedic texts like the revered Ashtanga Hridayam—has offered me a holistic understanding of the mind, body, and self. These timeless teachings help us cultivate clarity, focus, and inner balance. In today's fast-paced world, where digital lives heavily influence our thoughts, behaviours, and decisions, this ancient wisdom becomes even more essential. Rooted in these traditions, we will explore how one can navigate the digital world more securely, smoothly, and consciously—building inner resilience while addressing both internal and external challenges.

I thank my parents for their unwavering support and the values that have shaped my path. I am deeply grateful to my family for their constant encouragement and presence through every phase of this journey—this book is a reflection of their strength, patience, and inspiration. I also extend my heartfelt gratitude to Annamalai University at Chidambaram, where my journey into the profound world of Yoga deepened. Special thanks to the inspiring professors, especially the Director and Head Coordinator of the Yoga Department, and to my amazing classmates whose warm company, encouragement, and respectful collaboration enriched my learning experience

May the blessings of the Saptarishis and the guidance of Sage Patanjali illuminate your path as you delve into the pages of this book.

Salutations

मातृदेवो भव।

पितृदेवो भव।

आचार्यदेवो भव।

अतिथिदेवो भव।

Transliteration:

Mātṛ-devo bhava.

Pitṛ-devo bhava.

Ācārya-devo bhava.

Atithi-devo bhava.

Meaning:

"Regard your mother as God.

Regard your father as God.

Regard your teacher (guru) as God.

Regard your guest as God."

योगेन चित्तस्य पदेन वाचां

मलं शरीरस्य च वैद्यकेन।

योऽपाकरोत्तं प्रवरं मुनीनां

पतञ्जलिं प्राञ्जलिरानतोऽस्मि॥

Transliteration:

Yogena cittasya padena vācāṁ

Malaṁ śarīrasya ca vaidyakena,

Yo'pākarottaṁ pravaraṁ munīnāṁ

Patañjaliṁ prāñjalirānato'smi.

Meaning:

"I bow with folded hands to the revered sage Patanjali,

who gave us yoga for the purification of the mind,

grammar for the purity of speech,

and medicine (Ayurveda) for the health of the body."

Index

Chapter - 1

Understanding Security & Yoga in a Modern World

The Evolution of Security

Security has always been central to human survival, evolving alongside our societies, technologies, and fears. In ancient times, security was purely physical—protection from wild animals, natural disasters, and enemy tribes. Villages were built near rivers for resources and on high ground for defense. Walls, weapons, and warriors were the primary safeguards.

As civilizations advanced, so did the concept of security. Rulers built forts, armies, and systems of law to maintain order and protect people. Religion and culture also played a role—rituals, symbols, and beliefs were used to create a sense of protection from the unknown.

With the birth of cities and trade, new threats emerged: theft, deceit, and political instability. In response, laws became more sophisticated, policing was introduced, and surveillance methods began to form. Security became not just about fighting threats, but also about preventing them.

In the modern era, especially post-World Wars, security became a national and global concern. Nations built defense systems, intelligence agencies, and nuclear deterrents. Meanwhile, at the personal level, locks, ID cards, and alarm systems became everyday tools.

The digital age brought a new frontier: cybersecurity. With our lives moving online, threats shifted from physical to virtual—data theft, hacking, misinformation, and surveillance. Now, security means protecting both bodies and bytes.

Yet, despite all this progress, stress and fear have only increased. We have more tools, but less trust. More control, but less peace. This shows us that security must now evolve once more—not just outwardly, but inwardly. Beyond walls and firewalls, we must explore emotional, mental, and spiritual security. The next stage of evolution is not just smarter defense, but deeper understanding—of ourselves, of others, and of the systems we live in.

The Evolution of Yoga

Yoga, like security, has evolved over thousands of years, adapting to the needs of each era while staying rooted in timeless truths. Its origins trace back to the ancient Indus Valley civilization, where early forms of yogic postures and meditative symbols were found on seals and statues. In the **Vedic period**, yoga was primarily a spiritual discipline, focused on rituals, breath control (prāṇāyāma), and the pursuit of inner truth through devotion and discipline.

With the **Upanishads**, yoga deepened into a philosophy of unity—between the individual soul (*ātman*) and the universal spirit (*brahman*). The **Bhagavad Gita** later expanded yoga into multiple paths—**Karma Yoga** (action), **Bhakti Yoga** (devotion), and **Jnana Yoga** (knowledge)—making it accessible to people from different walks of life.

The classical system of yoga was compiled by **Sage Patanjali** in his *Yoga Sutras*, where he introduced the **Ashtanga Yoga** (eight-limbed path) for attaining mental clarity and liberation. Over time, yoga moved from the caves of monks into the hearts of daily life, especially during the medieval and modern periods, where Hatha Yoga brought more focus on physical postures and energy control.

In the **20th and 21st centuries,** yoga gained global recognition, often reshaped as a physical wellness practice. While it spread worldwide, its deeper purpose—self-awareness, mental stillness, and spiritual balance—remains its essence. Today, as stress and speed define modern

life, yoga is once again evolving—not as escape, but as a way to anchor ourselves in clarity, resilience, and peace.

Parallelism Between the Evolution of Security and Yoga

As security moved from swords to servers, yoga moved from solitude to society.

Both have evolved from outer defense to inner awareness—seeking peace not just through control, but through consciousness.

The Rise of Stress and Fear

In the past, stress and fear were rooted in immediate, physical threats—wild animals, hunger, wars, or natural disasters. Fear had a clear face, and stress was short-lived. Once the danger passed, the body and mind returned to balance. Life was uncertain, but people often lived in closer connection with nature, family, and community, which offered emotional grounding.

Today, the nature of fear has changed. It is no longer just about survival—it is subtle, constant, and often invisible. Modern stress comes not only from external threats, but from **information overload, social pressure, digital insecurity, job demands**, and a constant fear of "what might go wrong." Fear now travels through screens, pings, passwords, and headlines. Unlike in the past, where fear came in moments, modern fear is ongoing—it lingers in the mind and body, wearing down the nervous system.

Our world is more connected than ever, yet many feel isolated. We have more comfort, but less peace. We have more tools to protect ourselves, yet we often feel more unsafe. Fear has become mental and emotional—fueling anxiety, depression, burnout, and even conflict.

What changed? Our environment became faster than our minds could adapt. The speed of life outpaced the stillness within. We solved many outer problems, but we neglected the inner ones. That is why today's security challenge is not just about stopping harm from the outside—but about healing fear from the inside.

Recognizing this shift is the first step toward building a **stress-free** and **conscious** approach to security—where we don't just react to fear, but understand and transform it.

Where Technology Meets Vulnerability

Technology has changed the face of civilization. From instant communication to medical breakthroughs, from artificial intelligence to space exploration—human ingenuity has created tools once thought impossible. But as we marvel at our inventions, a difficult question arises: **If technology is progressing so rapidly, why do corruption, poverty, exploitation, and violence still exist?**

The answer lies in understanding a simple truth—**technology is a tool, not a compass**. It amplifies human capability, but not necessarily human character. A dishonest mind with powerful tools can do far more damage than ever before. A stressed society with advanced weapons or digital reach can spread fear faster than peace.

Technology has solved many *functional* problems—faster travel, efficient healthcare, global communication. But it hasn't yet solved our **essential human problems**: greed, fear, loneliness, ego, and disconnection. These are inner vulnerabilities that no device can fix. They live in the human mind and manifest in systems—through corrupt governance, manipulated media, unsafe products, and unjust battles.

In fact, the more powerful our technology becomes, the more dangerous our unresolved emotions and unconscious behaviors can be. A single line of malicious code can harm millions. A lie on social media can spark violence. A drone can replace a handshake.

This is where vulnerability meets power—and it's why we must evolve both. **We need inner clarity to guide outer capability.** Technology must be driven **by ethics, awareness, and compassion**. Without it, even the best inventions will only deepen division.

So, the real solution is not to reject technology—but to align it with wisdom. A stress-free, secure society cannot be built by **machines alone**. It must be shaped by **conscious humans using technology as an extension of inner balance—not a substitute for it**.

Modern world scenarios – The trigger of this book

Story #1

A story of silent burnout

In a modest middle-class household, parents poured their hopes and hard-earned savings into their child's future. They prioritized education above all else, believing it to be the key to stability and happiness. Their child worked diligently, earned a place at a prestigious national institution like IIT or NIT, and eventually landed a high-paying job at a top company.

With a generous salary, company perks like a personal laptop, cab facility, health benefits, and free cafeteria meals, life seemed perfect on the outside. Encouraged by this financial comfort, he made big decisions—he purchased a new car and bought a large house on a heavy loan, believing he had secured a future of long-term success.

For five years, he climbed the corporate ladder, built a strong bank balance, and appeared to live what many would call a dream life.

But beneath the surface, stress was building quietly. Long hours, irregular sleep, poor eating habits, and constant mental pressure began to take a toll. One day, routine medical tests revealed a harsh truth—he had developed chronic health conditions like diabetes and thyroid dysfunction. Though modern medicine provided temporary relief, the root causes remained unaddressed.

As the cycles of illness repeated, his medical expenses grew. The EMIs for his house and car added further pressure. His energy dropped, and gradually, his productivity declined. Despite his potential, he was now seen as a "poor performer." What once felt like a dream job began to feel like a burden. The same environment that once excited him now drained him.

His story is not uncommon. It reflects a growing reality where **external success masks internal imbalance**. When health, peace, and purpose are sacrificed in the pursuit of status or wealth, the cost is often greater than what the salary can cover.

Story #2

A champions fall

In a humble home filled with dreams, the parents took a path less traveled. Instead of pushing their son toward academic competition, they recognized his natural talent and passion for sports—especially badminton. With unwavering support, they encouraged him to train, persevere, and believe in himself.

Years of dedication, sweat, and sacrifice paid off. He rose through the ranks, representing the country on international courts. He became a **badminton world champion**, bringing pride to the nation and joy to his family. With success came **lavish rewards**—sponsorship deals, government cash prizes, media attention, and a life that felt larger than anything he had imagined.

But as the spotlight shone brighter, the shadows also grew. With sudden wealth, he bought a luxury apartment, a car, and began living a fast-paced lifestyle. The **rising cost of living**, **inflation**, and **high interest loans** soon began to bite into his savings. Worse still, **adulterated food** and **lack of nutritional discipline** began affecting his health and stamina.

Surrounded by the wrong circle of friends, and without a strong inner foundation or mentorship, he fell into habits that drained his energy and focus. The fame faded. The money slipped through his fingers. Slowly, without realizing, he had gone from a national hero to just another face in the crowd.

Now, he lives the life of a common man—earning just enough to get by, far from the courts and cameras.

Story #3

The fall of fame

He was a celebrated icon—an actor whose name lit up billboards and whose films touched millions. With years of fame and dedication to his craft, he earned **crores in wealth** and built a vast empire. From movies to endorsements, his fortune grew, and he invested it wisely—or so it seemed—by opening a **luxury shopping mall, makeup studios, salons**, and other lifestyle ventures.

At home, he lived in grandeur. His sprawling residence and business spaces were maintained by a team of **personal staff and workers** who managed everything from housekeeping to customer service. Life appeared flawless.

But slowly, cracks began to show.

One by one, the workers began to **fall ill**—suffering from pollution-related illnesses, **weakened immunity**, and health problems caused by **adulterated food and malnutrition**. Many of them came from vulnerable backgrounds, and as their health declined, they could no longer continue working. There was no one to take their place.

The absence of helping hands created disorder in the celebrity's daily life. **Stress levels rose**, routines broke down, and the once well-orchestrated system turned chaotic. Eventually, the pressure affected his own health. He was admitted to a top **super-speciality hospital**, but despite the best care, his condition worsened—and within days, he passed away.

The news shook the nation. Behind the glitz and glamour was a fragile reality.

His children, unprepared for such a sudden collapse, were left struggling to **cope with grief, confusion, and the responsibility** of rebuilding their lives. Once surrounded by luxury, they now faced uncertainty—trying to piece together a new normal from the remnants of a broken empire.

Story #4

A Daughter's Dilemma

In a quiet town, a middle-class couple lived with a single purpose—to give their only daughter the best life possible. They worked tirelessly, often sacrificing their own comforts to secure her education. The mother, especially, devoted herself fully to her daughter's upbringing. For nearly two decades, she put her own needs aside—**skipping meals, eating leftover food, ignoring rest**, and placing every ounce of energy into household chores and her child's growth.

She never complained. But time quietly took its toll.

Years of neglect led to a series of **chronic health issues—joint pain, thyroid imbalance, obesity, sciatica**, and **fatty liver disease**. Her eating habits—**irregular meals, cold water from the fridge, reheated food**—only worsened her condition. Yet, none of it seemed to matter the day they heard the news: their daughter had landed a **good IT job** in a major city. Their hard work had finally borne fruit.

But soon after, reality began to shift.

The mother's health declined rapidly. Alongside physical pain came **emotional stress and loneliness**—a silent ache from her daughter living far away. She began to **skip meals**, relied on **over-the-counter medications**, and gradually withdrew into fatigue and discomfort. Her worsening condition began to weigh heavily on her daughter's heart.

Miles away in the city, the daughter found it hard to concentrate at work. Each phone call brought anxiety. The very job that was meant to uplift the family now felt like a chain keeping her from her loved ones. Torn between career and caregiving, **she made a painful decision**—she resigned from her job and returned home to care for her mother.

The decision, though filled with love, came at a heavy cost. The family's **financial hopes were halted**, and much of their savings went into **ongoing medical care and treatments**. The dream they had worked so hard for slipped quietly into the background, replaced by the urgent reality of health and healing at home.

Story #5

The Taste That Turned Bitter

In the heart of a busy town, a small restaurant began drawing big crowds. Its menu was simple but irresistible—**golden samosas, crispy chips, masala vadas, medu vadas, mysore bondas, onion pakoras, kara bajjis**, and spicy fried snacks that filled the air with familiar aromas. Alongside, they served popular **junk food-style tiffins** like **greasy dosas loaded with ghee, deep-fried poori masala**, and **over-seasoned chutneys** that delighted the tongue.

Word spread fast. The restaurant became a favorite spot for locals, office-goers, and college students. Profits soared, and the owner expanded operations, hiring more cooks and helpers to meet the growing demand.

But over time, something began to change.

The crowds slowly thinned. Regular customers stopped returning. Day by day, the sales dipped. In an effort to cut costs, the owner reduced his staff. **Production declined**, and the once-buzzing kitchen began to fall silent. Eventually, he had no choice but to **shut down the business**.

The reason? A silent but serious oversight.

In his focus on taste and profit, the owner had ignored **basic hygiene and health practices**. He **reused cheap cooking oil**, neglected kitchen cleanliness, and paid no attention to the **quality or freshness of ingredients**. Over time, customers began experiencing **stomach issues, acidity, and infections**. Many, after visiting doctors, were **strictly advised to stop eating oily and unhygienic outside food**.

The trust was broken.

What had once brought joy became a source of harm. The same taste that had built his fame had also led to his fall. In the end, it wasn't a lack of customers, but a **lack of care** that shut the doors of his once-thriving restaurant.

Story #6

The Voice That Faded

He was a businessman with a heart rooted in social values. Beyond profits and markets, he dreamed of creating something meaningful—a platform that would uplift society. With his own investment and the support of like-minded friends, he launched a **news channel** driven by integrity and purpose.

He handpicked a team of **passionate journalists** who believed in honest storytelling. The channel became a rare voice, showcasing **positive stories** from across the state and country—**success journeys, grassroots innovations, acts of kindness, cultural values**, and real-life events filled with **morals and inspiration**. It wasn't just news; it was a celebration of the good in the world.

But slowly, their viewership started to decline.

Despite the quality of content and the sincerity behind their work, the ratings dropped. Not because they lacked talent or effort—but because the **media ecosystem around them was changing**. Competing channels began to **glorify negativity**, presenting crime, scandal, and controversy with **cinematic effects, suspenseful music, and dramatic visuals**. The audience shifted. **More screens turned to noise than to nuance**.

As revenue fell, the channel struggled to stay afloat. Advertisers moved toward higher TRP platforms. Salaries became harder to manage. The mission they had set out with—to build a channel that spread truth and positivity—faced the harsh reality of a marketplace that **rewarded sensation over substance**.

Eventually, the channel lost its financial footing. While their peers thrived on fear and spectacle, this honest voice faded—not due to failure in values, but due to **a lack of space for those values to survive** in the current media climate.

Story #7

When the Hero Crossed the Line

In the vast world of Indian cinema, there emerged a hero who captured the hearts of millions. Known for his gripping action scenes, deep emotional range, and mastery over the *Navarasa* — the nine emotional essences in Indian art — he wasn't just an actor, he became a phenomenon. His roles stood as symbols of righteousness, justice, and courage, and soon, he was elevated from a performer to a larger-than-life figure. Across the country, people didn't just admire him — they revered him.

As his fame grew, so did his influence. His fans began to see him not just as an entertainer, but as an embodiment of ideals — someone who reflected the kind of person they aspired to be. His fight against injustice, his honesty, his strength in adversity — all on screen — resonated deeply with the audience. For many, especially the youth, he became a moral compass, shaping their understanding of what is good, brave, and noble.

Then, quite unexpectedly, he began taking on villainous roles. These characters were dark, edgy, often violent — but brilliantly performed. His acting was praised, his box office success continued, and the industry celebrated his range and evolution. As an artist, he had clearly broken new ground. These roles, however, were not the typical black-and-white villains — they were layered, complex, sometimes even justifiable in their actions, fighting for causes in ways that challenged conventional law.

What followed was a subtle but noticeable shift among his audience. The very fans who once cheered for his heroism now found themselves rooting for his villainous characters. The actor's charisma, emotional depth, and familiar presence made these new roles appealing — almost noble. His actions, though outside the law or moral norms, were accepted — even admired — because they came from someone they had trusted for years as a symbol of virtue.

Over time, this began to blur the line between right and wrong in the minds of his followers. Young fans, especially, who had grown up seeing him as a hero, now began associating charm and strength with rebellion and violence. The distinction between heroism and villainy became increasingly vague. The very traits that once defined a villain — vengeance, manipulation, disregard for rules — were now seen as powerful, even attractive, simply because their favorite actor wore them with conviction.

This transformation, while celebrated artistically, created a shift in cultural perception that extended beyond cinema halls. A generation raised on his ideals was now being exposed to new definitions of power, success, and justice — ones that didn't necessarily align with the values he once portrayed. And through it all, the fanbase remained loyal, perhaps unaware of how their lens of good and bad was slowly being reshaped by the same face that had once defined their sense of what is right.

Story #8

Weekend Parenting

In the heart of a bustling metropolitan city, a modern couple lives a life that many would describe as successful. The husband works in a private firm, dedicated and driven, clocking long hours in pursuit of financial stability. The wife, equally ambitious, holds a comfortable position in the software industry. Together, they believe they are building a better future for their young children — a life filled with opportunities, comfort, and security.

On the surface, everything appears balanced. Both parents contribute financially. Their home is well-maintained, their children enrolled in reputed schools, and their weekends occasionally filled with quick getaways or mall visits. But underneath the routine, a different pattern is forming — one not immediately visible, but gradually shaping the emotional and moral fabric of the family.

The mother, while employed full-time, finds herself increasingly immersed in the social fabric of corporate life — lunch outings, team dinners, festive celebrations, birthday bashes, and light-hearted Friday activities. Her job, while professional, also becomes an avenue for personal freedom, a way to distance herself from the expectations of traditional homemaking. The idea of tending to in-laws or managing the children full-time feels like a compromise to her identity and autonomy.

Meanwhile, the father continues to stay absorbed in his workload, driven by deadlines, promotions, and performance metrics. By the time the weekend arrives, both parents are emotionally and physically drained. Their time with the children is limited, and within that small window, they prioritize affection over discipline. Conversations are filled with laughter, gifts, and indulgence, while uncomfortable topics — like school performance, discipline, manners, or values — are intentionally avoided.

What begins as a gesture of love slowly turns into a pattern. The parents, subconsciously aware of their absence during the week, choose to compensate with undivided affection during their limited time at home. But in doing so, they begin to silence the very questions that shape a child's character. There is no space for correction, no discussions on behaviour, no guidance on responsibilities — only a soft cocoon of unfiltered love.

As the days pass, the children grow within this one-dimensional emotional atmosphere — receiving affection without accountability, love without limits, freedom without feedback. While their basic needs are met and their parents' intentions are sincere, the absence of structured involvement in their emotional, moral, and behavioural growth quietly leaves a gap — a subtle but significant void that neither parent has paused to notice.

Story #9

Passion vs Pressure: Who Fixes the Fan Now?

In today's world, especially in India, students are often guided into conventional career paths like engineering or medicine, regardless of their personal interests. A majority now pursue fields such as Artificial Intelligence, driven by trends and societal expectations. Unfortunately, this has created a generation skilled in coding and algorithms, but unfamiliar with basic life skills—changing a tube light, fixing a fan, repairing a leaking or rusted tap, replacing a switch, or mending a bicycle or scooter.

As a result, even small household issues require calling professionals, leading to unnecessary expenses. Worse, the few skilled workers who can handle such jobs often switch to higher-paying desk jobs like real estate, accounting, or data entry. Their interest in hands-on work is lost, not because of lack of skill, but due to financial priorities.

However, imagine a world where a person becomes an electrician or plumber out of genuine passion. Regardless of wealth or status, such individuals would never refuse a repair request—they take joy in solving real-world problems. This highlights a deeper issue: when careers are driven by pressure instead of passion, both individuals and society lose. True progress lies in honoring and nurturing diverse talents—not just the academically prestigious ones.

Story #10

Talent Lost in Policy Blindness

A Heart-Touching Story of Talent Lost in Policy Blindness

Vedant was not just an employee—he was an asset whose brilliance elevated his entire IT team. During the pandemic, he worked remotely from his hometown Hyderabad, though officially based in Bangalore. From crisis management to client deliverables, Vedant's commitment never slipped. Clients trusted him. His teammates looked up to him. His contributions quietly strengthened the company's brand image.

Even after the pandemic, Vedant's productivity remained unmatched. But life had shifted—his elderly parents now relied on his care, and his children were well-settled in Hyderabad's schooling system. Though his company had a local office, policy demanded he return to Bangalore.

One day, Vedant was shocked to see his name on a "non-compliance" list—shared with HR and senior leaders. No one paused to ask *why*. No mechanism existed to assess whether such policies were still effective or damaging. His motivation declined. His passion faded. His manager expressed sympathy but was bound by rules: *"It's policy."*

Vedant resigned.

No one measured the aftershocks—team morale dipped, client satisfaction faltered, and delivery timelines stretched. Yet, no framework existed to scientifically analyze the cost of enforcing rigid policies versus the value of retaining top talent.

Vedant's departure wasn't just personal loss—it was a systemic failure to evolve. Had the organization used data to measure both employee realities and business outcomes, a win-win decision could've emerged.

In a world of change, policies must not be static—they must be intelligent, measurable, and humane

Story #11

The Illusion of Private Peace in a Publicly Unwell World

Imagine you are a successful businessman.

You've built your fortune by exporting natural resources from your homeland to wealthier nations. Your profits soared, your lifestyle upgraded, and now you live in a grand bungalow—high walls, manicured lawns, shimmering lights. You have everything money can buy.

But step outside the gates, and the reality is different. Unemployment is rising. Students around you are struggling to access basic education. Families live in cramped, unsafe homes. The roads are broken, the water isn't clean, the air feels heavier every day.

Still, you believe you've made it—you stay indoors, order everything online, immerse yourself in entertainment, thinking you're safe from the chaos outside.

But one day, the city falls sick.

A strange wave of illness spreads like wildfire. Your neighbors start coughing endlessly. The air is filled with the sound of ambulances. Entire families are bedridden. The people who once cleaned your house, cooked your meals, delivered your groceries, took care of your errands—no one shows up.

You wait a day, then two.

No groceries. No milk. No vegetables. No medicines. No domestic help. No plumber. No electrician. No driver. You have money, but no hands to help. You have a swimming pool, but no one to clean it. A grand dining hall, but nothing fresh to serve. A theater room, but nothing to celebrate.

Suddenly, the walls of your bungalow feel like barriers, not protection.

Luxury turns into loneliness. Wealth into helplessness.

It dawns on you—**your happiness was never yours alone.**

It was built silently on the health of your environment and the well-being of the people around you.

You were only as secure as the world outside your window.

- No man lives in isolation.
- If the air around you is poisoned, your breath cannot be pure.
- If your neighbors are unwell, your peace cannot be real.
- If society is collapsing, your success cannot stand tall for long.

True security is not how much you own, but how much wellness you share with the world around you.

S.No	Story Title	Summary	Moral / Core Insight
Story #1	**A Story of Silent Burnout**	A successful IT professional with high pay falls sick due to poor lifestyle and stress.	Success without health awareness leads to silent suffering and collapse.
Story #2	**A Champion's Fall**	A sports star loses wealth and health due to lack of discipline and wrong influences.	Talent and fame require ongoing discipline and right company to sustain success.
Story #3	**The Fall of Fame**	A celebrity's staff fall ill, affecting his life and business, leading to his own decline.	One's ecosystem matters—neglecting community well-being can backfire personally.
Story #4	**A Daughter's Dilemma**	A daughter quits her job to care for her sick mother whose health was long ignored.	Family sacrifices can come full circle; ignoring health has generational consequences.

Story #5	**The Taste That Turned Bitter**	A popular snack shop closes due to unhealthy practices and customer health issues.	Profits built on unhealthy habits cannot last—people value trust and safety.
Story #6	**The Voice That Faded**	A good-news media channel shuts down due to lack of public interest amid sensationalism.	Truthful, positive efforts struggle when society rewards noise over value.
Story #7	**When the Hero crossed the line**	Influence shapes perception; when ideals change onscreen, audience values unconsciously shift in real life.	Great influence carries silent responsibility — entertainment should not erode society's understanding of right and wrong.
Story **#8**	**Weekend Parenting**	Emotional presence is not just about love — children need consistent guidance, correction, and engagement for holistic growth.	In chasing dreams and showing love, parents must not forget their role in shaping values, discipline, and deeper connection.
Story #9	**Passion vs Pressure: Who Fixes the Fan Now?**	Pursuing careers without passion creates a society lacking basic skills, leading to dependency and unnecessary expenses.	When passion guides work, every task gains purpose; when pressure dictates it, even simple needs remain unfulfilled.

Story #10	**Talent Lost in Policy Blindness**	A loyal, high-performing employee leaves due to rigid policies, highlighting a system blind to human needs.	Policies must be measured scientifically for their impact on people and business, enabling data-driven, win-win decisions.
Story #11	**The Illusion of Private Peace in a Publicly Unwell World**	True peace comes not from wealth, but from the collective health and well-being of your surrounding environment.	Your happiness and security depend on the health and well-being of the people and environment around you.

Chapter - 2

Physical Security — The Outer Shell

Personal Safety: Guarding the Self

- **The Body as the First Temple**: In yoga, the body is considered a sacred vessel. Just as we cleanse and protect temples, physical safety begins with honouring and caring for the body.
- **Situational Awareness as Mindfulness**: Awareness of surroundings can be seen as an extension of yogic *pratyahara*—the conscious withdrawal and redirection of the senses. It's not about fear, but about conscious, alert presence.
- **Healthy Boundaries**: Just as *asanas* establish balance and posture, establishing personal boundaries in life (physical space, relationships, time) mirrors this principle off the mat.

- **Fight or Flight vs. Yogic Calm**: The body's stress response is natural but can be refined through breathwork (*pranayama*) and regular meditation to avoid hypervigilance or dissociation.

Family Security: Building Safe Havens

- **The Home as an Ashram**: Security isn't just about locks and alarms—it's about cultivating a sanctuary where love, trust, and grounded energy thrive.
- **Shared Mindfulness**: Collective practices like family yoga or mindful meals promote emotional bonding, which is itself a layer of invisible security.
- **Teach, Don't Instill Fear**: In yogic parenting, the goal is *shiksha* (teaching with love), not control through fear. Preparing family members with awareness and calm decision-making builds resilience.

Community and Border Security: Collective Protection

- **Security Without Separation**: The yogic view of *Vasudhaiva Kutumbakam* ("The world is one family") suggests that true security doesn't arise from isolation but from collective harmony.
- **Sacred Space for All**: Public safety measures should be inclusive, not alienating. Community-led initiatives with compassion can often succeed where authoritarianism fails.
- **Energetic Borders vs. Physical Borders**: Yogis understand that protection can be energetic as well as physical. Just as an aura can be cleared and strengthened, communities can reinforce safety through spiritual and social cohesion.

Pitfalls: Over-Securitization, Surveillance, and Anxiety

- **Fear-Based Security Breeds More Fear**: When protection becomes paranoia, we're reinforcing the very mental stress that yoga seeks to dissolve.

- **Surveillance Is Not Presence**: True presence is embodied awareness, not constant observation. Surveillance might catch a moment, but it can't foster connection or trust.
- **Hyper-Protection Disempowers**: Over-securitization leads to dependency and helplessness. In yogic terms, it disconnects us from our inner *shakti*—our inherent strength and autonomy.

Yogic Insights: Grounding, Presence, and Fearlessness

- **Root Chakra (Muladhara) as the Foundation**: Physical security aligns with the root chakra. Practices that ground us—like walking barefoot, connecting with the Earth, deep squats—reinforce our sense of physical and psychological safety.
- **Presence as the Ultimate Protection**: Fear often arises from projections into the future. Through *dharana* (focused attention), we become alert and calm in the now.
- **Fearlessness (*Abhaya*) as a Yogic Ideal**: The yogic warrior is not aggressive but fearless. Security, when approached through yoga, is not about control but about liberation from fear.
- **Breathe into Safety**: A simple deep breath, especially using techniques like *nadi shodhana* (alternate nostril breathing), can instantly reset the nervous system and bring a felt sense of safety.

Chapter - 3

Digital Security — The Inner Web

What Is Digital Security?

Reality First:

Digital security is the protection of data, systems, and networks in an interconnected digital world. It includes safeguarding against cyber threats, data breaches, identity theft, and manipulation. For individuals and organizations alike, digital security has become foundational—touching everything from finances to health records to national defense. Yet, it's invisible, fast-evolving, and complex—making it both vital and mentally taxing.

Yogic Insight:

In yoga, the inner world is woven with networks of *nadis*—energy channels carrying *prana* (life force), much like how information flows through digital networks. Just as blockages in the subtle body cause disharmony, vulnerabilities in digital systems threaten overall stability. Security in the digital world, like health in the subtle body, requires regular purification, awareness, and ethical flow. Mastery begins with awareness—not only of external tools, but of inner patterns.

Information Security: Data, Privacy, and Protection

Reality First:

Information is the new currency—data about who we are, what we do, and how we think. From social media to surveillance capitalism, our digital footprints are constantly being tracked, analyzed, and monetized. This creates a dual concern: protecting private data from bad actors, and understanding the deeper implications of always being watched.

Yogic Insight:

In yogic philosophy, inner knowledge (*jnana*) is to be guarded and respected. Just as a sage shares wisdom with discretion, we must treat personal data as sacred. The principle of *ahimsa* (non-harming) extends to digital ethics—harming someone through breaches, leaks, or unwanted surveillance is karmically no different than physical harm. And *pratyahara*, the withdrawal of senses, reminds us to selectively engage with stimuli—choosing what we share, and with whom.

Product Security: Building Safe Digital Systems

Reality First:

Product security involves designing software and systems that are resistant to exploitation. It requires foresight, testing, threat modeling, and a deep understanding of both user behavior and attacker mindset. Developers are constantly racing against evolving threats. Yet often, systems are built with speed and profit in mind, rather than safety and ethics.

Yogic Insight:

Yoga teaches conscious design through *intelligent action*—what is called *karma yoga*. Building secure systems is akin to creating an asana: structurally balanced, energetically aligned, and able to withstand stress. A secure digital product isn't just a technical success; it's a reflection of inner values—*saucha* (purity), *tapas* (discipline), and *svadhyaya* (self-study). Systems, like humans, must be designed to adapt, defend, and remain clear in purpose.

Pitfalls: Hyper Vigilance, Burnout, and Paranoia

Reality First:

Digital security professionals live under a continuous threat model—always anticipating the next breach, patch, or incident. The pace is relentless, with no real "off switch." This leads to hypervigilance, decision fatigue, sleep disturbances, and burnout. Over time, it's easy to slip into paranoia or detachment, feeling disconnected from the human side of the systems being protected.

Yogic Insight:

In yoga, this is the state of excessive *rajas*—a mind overactive and agitated, constantly spinning. The solution isn't to push harder, but to restore *sattva*—equilibrium. Stress in digital security doesn't arise solely from external threats, but from the mind's resistance to uncertainty. Yogic tools such as *asana*, *pranayama*, and *dhyana* (meditation) calm the nervous system and create a spacious awareness, enabling clarity without anxiety. Paranoia dissolves when *viveka* (discernment) replaces fear-driven thinking.

Yogic Tools: Clarity, Focus, and Detachment

Reality First:

In a digital world full of noise—constant notifications, security alerts, misinformation, and fear-based decision-making—what's most needed is clear perception, sustained attention, and the ability to detach from distractions. Without these inner capacities, digital security becomes reactive and fragile.

Yogic Insight:

Yoga offers exactly what the digital mind lacks:

- **Clarity** (*sattva*) through meditation, which stills the mind and clears emotional fog.
- **Focus** (*dharana*) through mindful breath and posture, training attention like a laser.
- **Detachment** (*vairagya*) not as withdrawal, but as freedom from compulsive attachment—whether to data, results, control, or fear.

Just as a firewall filters harmful intrusions, a yogic mindset filters mental clutter. It protects the practitioner from internal malware—doubt, restlessness, craving—so that digital responsibility is handled with serenity, not stress.

Chapter - 4

Scenarios of Stress in Security Roles

The Ethical Hacker's Anxiety

Reality First:

Ethical hackers, often portrayed as digital heroes, live in a high-pressure world. They're expected to think like malicious actors, constantly scan for vulnerabilities, and carry the weight of protecting systems from invisible threats. This role demands deep concentration, rapid response, and often a sense of isolation—working in the shadows of both legality and morality. There's always the risk of missing something critical. The "what-if" culture breeds constant unease.

Yogic Perspective:

This mirrors the mental restlessness described in yoga as *chitta vritti*—fluctuations of the mind. The hacker is mentally dispersed, pulled in many directions by simulated threats. *Dharana* (focused concentration) and *pranayama* (breath control) can offer tools to reclaim mental stillness. The ethical hacker, like a yogi, must operate in the shadows yet remain internally clear, ethical, and steady—anchored in *satya* (truth) and *viveka* (discernment).

The Border Guard's Dilemma

Reality First:

A border guard is the embodiment of physical security, caught at the intersection of geopolitics, migration, and law enforcement. The dilemma arises when compassion clashes with orders. Guards may face families seeking asylum, refugees fleeing terror, or individuals crossing for survival. This role is emotionally taxing—requiring enforcement of boundaries, sometimes against personal values.

Yogic Perspective:

This inner conflict reflects *dharma sankata*—a moral crossroads, well known in texts like the *Bhagavad Gita*, where Arjuna is paralyzed by the ethics of war. Border guards, like Arjuna, need clarity on what action is aligned with higher duty (*dharma*), not just policy. Practices of *self-inquiry* and *karma yoga* (action without attachment) can help bring peace to those forced into hard choices.

The CISO's Sleepless Nights

Reality First:

Chief Information Security Officers (CISOs) are burdened with the responsibility of protecting the entire digital framework of an organization. A single breach can have catastrophic effects—financially, legally, and reputationally. They live with constant accountability, face technical overload, human error, regulatory compliance, and limited resources. It's a lonely, high-stakes position. Sleep loss and burnout are common.

Yogic Perspective:

This unrelenting mental pressure is *rajasic*—driven by activity, ambition, and overstimulation. The antidote is cultivating *sattva*—clarity, calm, and steadiness. Through meditation (*dhyana*), a CISO can learn to respond instead of react, to witness the pressure without being consumed. *Yoga Nidra* (yogic sleep) can be particularly healing—replacing depleted rest with deep, restorative awareness.

The Family Man with Surveillance Worries

Reality First:

In a world of smart devices, tracking apps, and cameras, the average person—especially a parent or caregiver—can become consumed with protecting their family from perceived digital and physical threats. Surveillance starts with good intent but can escalate into fear, mistrust, and even obsession. Constant monitoring of children, partners, or the home can create emotional distance and internal stress.

Yogic Perspective:

This scenario represents a grasping for control—what yoga calls *avidya* (ignorance of the true nature of reality) and *abhinivesha* (clinging to life/fear of death). Yoga teaches that true safety is not achieved by controlling every outcome but by cultivating presence, trust, and intuition. *Aparigraha* (non-possessiveness) and *shraddha* (faith) can shift the protector's mindset from fear-based control to love-based guidance.

Inner Reflection: Where Stress is Born

Reality First:

Across these roles, stress isn't just external—it arises from within. The pressure to be perfect, the fear of failure, moral ambiguity, over-responsibility, and hyper-vigilance all originate in the mind. In security roles, this stress is often internalized and rarely expressed, making it more toxic over time. The cost is emotional exhaustion, relationship strain, and identity confusion.

Yogic Perspective:

Yoga identifies the root of suffering as *kleshas*—ignorance, ego, attachment, aversion, and fear. Security roles amplify these mental patterns unless we are conscious. Stress is not just a reaction to threat, but a signal to explore where our identity, expectations, and fears are misaligned. Through regular *svadhyaya* (self-study) and *sadhana* (spiritual practice), individuals can reconnect with a centered, expansive identity—not defined by roles or responsibilities, but by stillness and self-awareness.

Chapter - 5

The Yogic Lens — Inner Security First

What is Yogic Security?

- **Security is a state of being, not a set of conditions.** In yoga, true security (*shanti*, inner peace) arises not from external defenses, but from a deep sense of grounded self-awareness.
- **Yogic security is inner steadiness amidst outer change.** It's the *muladhara chakra* (root energy center) fully activated—

where you feel rooted in your body, values, and presence, no matter what happens around you.

- **It is freedom from fear, not freedom from threat.** The yogic seeker understands that fear is not dissolved by controlling the world, but by realizing the Self (*Atman*)—unchanging, whole, and eternal.
- **Inner security is the foundation for ethical action.** When you are stable within, you act with compassion, clarity, and courage rather than control, aggression, or reactivity.

The Power of Breath and Awareness

- **The breath is the bridge.** Between body and mind, between reaction and response. It is the first and most reliable tool to shift from anxiety to presence.
- **Every breath is a choice.** Shallow breathing feeds panic. Deep, conscious breathing rewires the nervous system from fight-or-flight (*sympathetic*) to rest-and-restore (*parasympathetic*).
- **Awareness (*smriti* or mindfulness) creates space.** The space between stimulus and response is where security lives—not in the reaction, but in the conscious pause.
- **Pranayama is psychic hygiene.** Just as we protect data with firewalls, *pranayama* protects your inner environment from toxic thoughts, overstimulation, and emotional volatility.

From Control to Connection

- **Control is a fear response. Connection is a trust response.** When we try to control everything—people, outcomes, systems—we are reacting from the root fear of loss or harm.
- **Yoga teaches surrender (*Ishvarapranidhana*), not passivity.** It is the surrender of egoic control and the embrace of connected, purposeful engagement.

- **Security grows through relationship.** Through *bhakti* (devotion), *seva* (service), and *sangha* (community), we remember we are not isolated agents but part of a greater fabric.
- **Connection is inner attunement.** When you are in tune with your body, breath, and intuition, you don't need to monitor every external variable—you simply respond from aligned wisdom.

Practices to Build Resilience

- **Resilience is the ability to return to center.** It's not about being unshaken, but about regaining balance quickly after disturbance.
- **Daily sadhana creates inner reserves.** Regular spiritual practice builds energetic immunity—protecting your mental clarity and emotional stamina like an armor of *ojas* (vitality).
- **Asana grounds the body.** Poses like Tadasana (Mountain Pose), Balasana (Child's Pose), and Virabhadrasana (Warrior Pose) cultivate rooted strength and emotional courage.
- **Meditation sharpens perception.** Just 10–20 minutes a day rewires your nervous system and builds the "observer mind" that doesn't get hijacked by panic or pressure.
- **Mantra reinforces inner structure.** Sound vibrations like *Om*, *So Hum*, or *Lokah Samastah Sukhino Bhavantu* anchor the mind to a higher, stabilizing frequency.

Stillness in the Face of Uncertainty

- **Stillness is not inactivity—it's conscious presence.** It's the quiet inner center from which all skillful action arises.
- **Uncertainty is a given. Inner stillness is a choice.** The yogi does not demand certainty from life. Instead, they cultivate unwavering awareness in the midst of chaos.
- **The eye of the storm is within you.** No matter how turbulent the outer world becomes—cyber threats, political unrest, personal loss—the yogic path returns you to the calm center.

- **True protection is presence.** When you are fully present, fear loses its grip. Security professionals and seekers alike can embody this stillness as their greatest shield.

Chapter - 6

Bridging Both Worlds — Practical Meets Spiritual

Designing Systems with Conscious Awareness

Security isn't just about firewalls and protocols; it begins with the consciousness behind the creation. Just as a yogi enters each asana with intention and alignment, a security professional must design systems with awareness—not from fear, but from clarity.

Drawing inspiration from *Samyama* (the fusion of Dharana, Dhyana, and Samadhi), conscious system design means:

- Intuiting vulnerabilities before they manifest.
- Balancing robustness with user well-being.
- Creating frameworks that respect human dignity and freedom, rather than merely enforcing control.

Just as the mind must be trained to stay in harmony with the Self, systems must be built in harmony with their users and the environments they serve.

Mindful Monitoring: Alert, Not Anxious

Yoga teaches us to be the *sakshi* (witness), observing without attachment. In security, monitoring systems often tip into obsession and hyper-vigilance, breeding burnout and stress.

Mindful monitoring means:

- Staying alert without being reactive.
- Watching trends and behaviors like a yogi watches breath—attentive, calm, and clear.
- Responding, not overreacting.

When the mind is trained to witness rather than wander, we begin to see clearly and act decisively. This same principle reduces false alarms, improves threat detection, and promotes balance in security operations.

Leadership in Security with Compassion

True yogic leadership emerges from *Ahimsa* (non-violence), *Satya* (truth), and *Karuna* (compassion). The modern security landscape, often driven by control and punishment, can learn much from this.

Leading with compassion in security involves:

- Empowering teams rather than instilling fear.
- Building a culture of trust and responsibility instead of blame.
- Understanding that mistakes are part of learning, just as falling is part of asana practice.

When leaders embody yogic values, they create environments that are not only secure but also psychologically safe.

Yogic Ethics Applied to Cyber and Physical Domains

The *Yamas* and *Niyamas* are not just personal guidelines—they are foundational for creating secure, ethical spaces.

- **Ahimsa (Non-violence):** Avoiding harm through intrusive surveillance or exploitative policies.
- **Satya (Truth):** Transparent communication in incident responses and policy development.
- **Asteya (Non-stealing):** Respecting data privacy and intellectual property.
- **Aparigraha (Non-possessiveness):** Avoiding over-collection of user data.
- **Saucha (Purity):** Keeping systems clean, updated, and uncluttered.
- **Tapas (Discipline):** Maintaining vigilance and regular security drills.

When these principles are embedded in both policy and practice, the boundary between the spiritual and the practical dissolves.

Chapter – 7

The Role of A.I. in Stress-Free Security

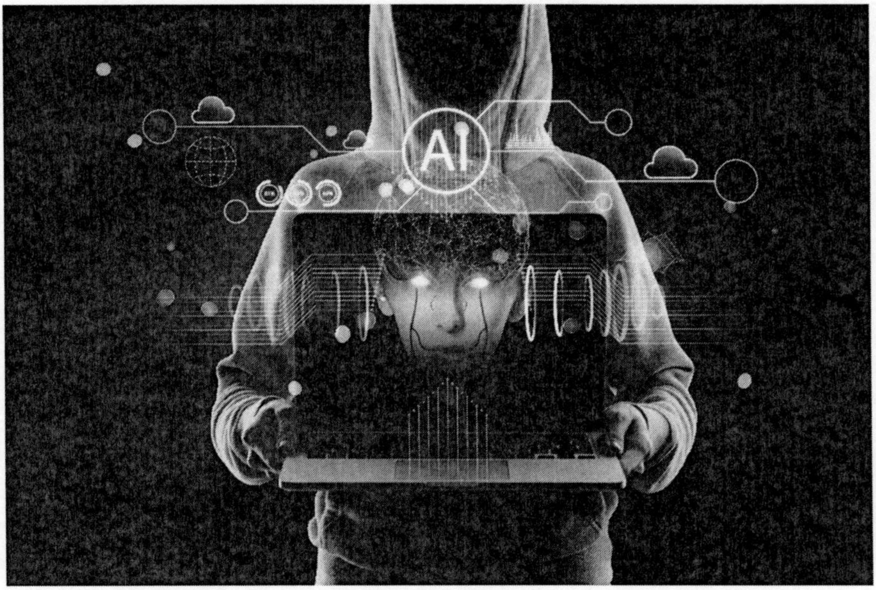

How A.I. is Transforming Security

- Predictive Intelligence: A.I. enhances security by detecting patterns, anomalies, and potential threats before they manifest—mirroring the yogic idea of *pratiprasava* (reversing the modifications of the mind) to prevent disturbances before they surface.
- Vigilance Without Fatigue: Unlike human guards or analysts, A.I. operates without sleep or distraction, embodying *abhyāsa* (constant practice) which Patanjali defines as necessary for stability of mind.

- Expanded Awareness: Advanced systems replicate the function of *dṛṣṭā* (the Seer), observing without judgment—this parallels yogic mindfulness and silent witnessing.
- Reducing Physical Burden: Automating surveillance, data analysis, and threat response reduces physical and cognitive stress for humans—offering the potential for a "security without suffering" model.

Pitfalls of Over-Reliance and Control

- Attachment (*Rāga*) to Control: Over-reliance on A.I. reflects a subtle attachment to control outcomes. In Yoga Sutras, attachment is one of the *kleshas* (afflictions) that leads to suffering.
- Disempowerment of Human Intuition: Constant deferral to machines may dull our *viveka* (discrimination) and *buddhi* (higher intelligence), weakening internal alertness.
- Illusion of Certainty (*Avidyā*): Blind trust in algorithms creates *avidyā*—ignorance of the true nature of things—mistaking data-driven output for complete truth.
- Ethical Drift: Systems without conscious anchoring can become tools of oppression rather than protection, violating *ahimsā* (non-violence) and *satya* (truthfulness).

A.I. and Human Emotion: Where Tension Grows

- Emotional Surveillance: A.I.'s ability to read facial expressions, tone, and micro-expressions can feel invasive, creating psychological stress and a subconscious sense of being watched—contrary to the yogic pursuit of *swarajya* (self-governance).
- The Illusion of Empathy: Machines simulating compassion without consciousness can trigger dissonance in humans, making emotional connection feel synthetic or manipulative.

- Amplification of Bias and Fear: When A.I. responds to human fear patterns, it can perpetuate threat-based thinking—contrary to *chitta prasādana* (peaceful mind).
- Misalignment with Human Energy: A system unaware of *prāṇa* (life force) and *sattva* (clarity/purity) may operate in a high-tension state, increasing stress even in the name of security.

Coexistence: Building Trust between Human and Machine

- Mutual Respect Over Control: Like in *guru-shishya* relationships, the human-A.I. interaction should be one of mutual respect and guidance—not domination.
- Transparency as *Satya*: Clear algorithms, transparent data practices, and open feedback loops reflect the yogic principle of truthfulness.
- Integrating Stillness into Design: Just as a yogi finds calm between breaths, systems can be designed with 'breathing space'—delays, pauses, and feedback periods to reduce urgency and stress.
- Conscious Co-Creation: Bringing together *manas* (mind), *buddhi* (intellect), and machine intelligence in a balanced way allows for evolution without tension—true *sangha* (cohesive community).

A Yogic Framework for Designing Ethical A.I. Systems

- Yamas and Niyamas as Ethical Code:
    - *Ahimsā*: Prevent harm by bias-checking and avoiding manipulative designs.
    - *Satya*: Transparency in decision-making algorithms.
    - *Asteya*: Avoid data theft or unauthorized usage.
    - *Brahmacharya*: Channel technology towards higher purpose.

  - *Aparigraha*: Avoid hoarding data; only collect what's needed.

- Sādhana in System Tuning: Regular updates and mindful retraining of A.I. models mirrors the yogic path of *sādhana* (disciplined practice).
- Balancing Gunas: A Sattvic system fosters harmony, Rajasic systems may chase speed, and Tamasic ones might be sluggish or harmful. Designing for *sattva* increases collective peace.
- Inner Security First: A system cannot truly ensure outer safety if its creators and users are internally stressed. As inside, so outside—*yatha antar, tatha bahir*.

Use of A.I. and Robotics in High-Risk Human Security Roles

1. **Preserving Human Life**: Deploying humanoid robots in conflict zones or hostile borders can minimize the death toll among soldiers—honoring the yogic principle of *ahimsā* (non-harming).
2. **Predictive Surveillance**: A.I.-powered drones and cameras can detect patterns of movement, infiltration, or enemy buildup—providing early warnings and reducing surprise attacks (*pratiprasava* in action).
3. **Neutral, Unemotional Decision-Making**: Machines can respond without panic or revenge, avoiding escalation in emotionally charged situations—aligning with *sthita prajna* (stable intellect).
4. **Reduced Mental Burden on Soldiers**: By offloading high-risk monitoring to machines, soldiers can retain better emotional balance and avoid PTSD—enhancing *chitta prasādana* (peace of mind).
5. **Around-the-Clock Vigilance**: A.I. doesn't require rest, food, or morale boosts, ensuring 24x7 alertness without fatigue—embodying the tireless *abhyāsa* of a committed yogi.

6. **Remote-Controlled or Autonomous Response Systems**: Dangerous areas like minefields or terrorist hotspots can be patrolled by A.I.-driven robots, safeguarding human lives.
7. **Minimizing Errors from Stress or Fatigue**: Unlike human guards who may be distracted, tired, or emotionally compromised, robots maintain consistent performance.
8. **Monitoring Physiological and Energetic States**: A.I. can detect not only physical threats but also psychological or energetic disturbances in soldiers—supporting *prāṇa* regulation and mental well-being.
9. **Protection Without Aggression**: Defensive systems designed with a yogic approach can neutralize threats non-lethally—via immobilization or deterrence instead of destruction.
10. **Humanoid Guards with Compassion Algorithms**: Robots infused with ethical constraints (e.g., *do no harm*, *empathize before act*) could represent sattvic (harmonious) warriors.
11. **Sensorial Multiplicity**: Robotic guards can have thermal vision, night vision, vibration detection, and audio triangulation—offering *expanded perception* beyond human limitations.
12. **AI-Assisted Border Control**: Combining satellite data, drone patrols, and ground robotics can create intelligent borders that adapt in real time—embodying *viveka khyāti* (discernment with clarity).
13. **A.I. Companion Systems for Soldiers**: Emotionally aware robots could offer real-time support, meditation cues, breathing reminders, or grounding exercises in stressful situations—yogic tools in machine form.
14. **Ethical Combat Design**: If conflict becomes unavoidable, A.I. can be programmed to prioritize minimal damage, surrender prompts, and ceasefire options—respecting *dharma* over destruction.

15. **Spiritual Warrior Ethos in Code**: Inspired by the *Bhagavad Gita*, code can be written to ensure robots protect *dharma*, not just territory—infusing machines with higher purpose, not blind obedience.

Chapter - 8

A Vision for the Future

What a Stress-Free Secure World Looks Like

- **Security Rooted in Awareness, Not Arms**: In such a world, the foundation of safety is not weaponry but *vigilant awareness*—where *yoga chitta vritti nirodhah* (stilling the fluctuations of the mind) becomes a social norm.

- **Harmonious Coexistence Over Competition**: Societies move from "defending borders" to "expanding bonds." This echoes *samadhi*—union, where division loses meaning.

- **Technology as a Reflection of Consciousness**: Machines are designed and deployed not just for efficiency but with *sattva*—

clarity, purity, balance. AI becomes a tool of compassion and precision, not control.

- **Holistic Infrastructure**: Cities integrate meditation spaces, nature, clean energy, ethical governance, and digital ethics—blending *sharira (body)*, *manas (mind)*, and *atma (spirit)* into daily living.
- **Global Dharma-Based Governance**: Policies are no longer reactive to threats but proactive toward balance—modeled on *dharma-sankat* resolutions as found in Gita and yogic ethics.

From Fear-Based to Trust-Based Security

- **Replacing Suspicion with *Shraddha* (Inner Faith)**: Instead of operating from fear and paranoia, systems are built around *shraddha*—confidence in human potential and divine order.
- **Security as a Flow, Not a Fortress**: Like breath (*prāṇāyāma*), security is seen as rhythm—expanding, pausing, and contracting with consciousness, not rigidity.
- **Community Vigilance Over Surveillance State**: People become self-aware and socially responsible, much like *yamas and niyamas* guiding inner and outer conduct.
- **Transparency as Trust Technology**: Open algorithms, accountable governance, and emotional honesty replace secrecy, manipulation, and mistrust.
- **Leadership by Seers, Not Controllers**: The future belongs to leaders with inner clarity, like *rishis*—who lead by insight, not intimidation.

Teaching the Next Generation

- **Spiritual Intelligence in School Curricula**: Alongside AI and coding, children learn *viveka* (discernment), *vairagya* (non-attachment), *pratyāhāra* (sense mastery)—tools for inner stability.

- **From Examination to Realization**: Assessment systems evolve to test for awareness, empathy, creative problem solving, and inner peace—not rote learning.
- **Yoga as Life Science, Not an Exercise**: Children are taught asanas, yes—but also the subtle energies, breath regulation, silence, and the power of focused thought (*dhyana*).
- **Children as Peace Ambassadors**: Youth grow up with a mindset of global harmony, seeing the world as *vasudhaiva kutumbakam* (one family), not as zones of threat.
- **Digital Ethics as Core Education**: Children are made aware of how to use A.I. responsibly, protect privacy, and honor truth online—developing digital *satya*.

Inner Peace as the Ultimate Security

- **Stillness as Strength**: Inner silence (*mauna*) becomes more powerful than alarms and fences. People no longer react—they *respond* from centered awareness.
- **No Inner Enemy, No Outer War**: When people resolve internal conflict—jealousy, fear, greed—external wars lose their fuel.
- **The End of "Us vs Them" Thinking**: The yogic realization of *purusha* (universal Self) dissolves dualities. No threat remains when separation disappears.
- **Inner Peace as a Civic Metric**: Future societies may measure success not just by GDP but by *inner peace index*—mental health, joy, cooperation, and sense of belonging.
- **Security as Seva (Service)**: The highest form of protection is *seva*—where people feel so connected, they naturally act to protect one another's well-being.

Yogic Security Is Not Passive — It Is Proactive, But Rooted in Clarity

- Yogic teachings do not ask us to abandon action (*karma*); they ask us to act from stillness, not fear. The *Bhagavad Gita* was spoken on a battlefield.
- A soldier who trains in awareness, breath control, and emotional stability will make fewer fear-based decisions under pressure, and may save lives—including their own.

Yoga Enhances the Soldier, It Doesn't Replace the Soldier

- Yogic practices can:
  - Sharpen perception and reflexes (through *pratyāhāra, dhāraṇā*)
  - Regulate the nervous system under extreme stress (through *prāṇāyāma*)
  - Help recover from trauma, burnout, and loss (through *dhyāna* and *satvik routines*)
- This doesn't make a soldier less effective—it makes them more *resilient*, *precise*, and *mentally fit*. Many elite units worldwide (even special forces) now incorporate mindfulness and breathwork in training.

AI + Yogic Intelligence = Nonviolent Power

- The **goal is not to disarm**, but to **replace direct violence with intelligent defense**—using predictive A.I., robotics, satellite monitoring, drone patrols, and automated deterrent systems.
- Soldiers and police become *guardians*, not just fighters—more like *kṣatriyas* (warriors with dharmic ethics).
- You prevent enemies not just by overpowering them—but by *seeing before they strike*, *understanding their motives*, and *disarming situations before they escalate*. That's yoga in national defense.

Prevention Is Greater Than Retaliation

- Yoga teaches *pratipaksha bhavana*—countering negative tendencies with positive awareness. This can be applied at a **policy level**.
- Diplomacy, cultural intelligence, cyber-defense, and social integration are part of a **holistic security strategy**, not just military strength.

Inner Stability Leads to Better Leadership in Government and Defense

- When leaders in the military or police cultivate inner calm and clarity, they:
  - Make more ethical, long-term decisions
  - Avoid aggression from ego
  - Build trust within and across borders
- Leadership programs integrating yogic values (not just techniques) can shape visionary commanders and administrators.

Summary

Real Security: Preventing the Need for Retaliation

In traditional geopolitics, when Country **ABC** harms or attacks Country **XYZ**, the immediate expectation is **retaliation**—a military or economic response to demonstrate strength, restore balance, or deter future aggression.

But here lies the yogic insight:

The need for retaliation indicates that security has already failed.

From a **yogic standpoint**, the entire chain of events—harm, victimhood, retaliation—is **a cycle of reaction born from unawareness**. Just as in the human mind, where a thought left unchecked becomes an emotion, and emotion becomes impulsive action—so too in global affairs, **ignorance breeds conflict**.

Retaliation is a Costly Teacher—Yogic Foresight is a Compassionate Guardian

If Country XYZ had adopted a **Yogic Security Model**, this is what could have been different:

1. **Continuous Awareness (*satarkata*)**

   Through A.I.-assisted surveillance, energy mapping, geopolitical insight, and local intelligence, potential threats would have been **seen before they surfaced**.

2. **Energetic & Emotional Intelligence (*chitta shuddhi*)**

   By monitoring not just physical borders but **internal unrest**—within ABC or radicalized factions—XYZ could have engaged in **non-violent disruption**, diplomacy, or humanitarian pre-intervention.

3. **No Victimhood, No Revenge**

   In yoga, the moment you say "I am harmed," you give up your power.

   The moment you say "I will harm in return," you perpetuate the cycle.

   The yogic approach is to prevent both.

4. **Response, Not Reaction**

   If retaliation is necessary, it must come from **dharmic discernment**, not rage. A response guided by *viveka* (wisdom), not vengeance, can neutralize threat **with minimal collateral damage**—both physically and karmically.

5. **Saving Lives, Saving Resources**

   Retaliation always comes at a cost—human, economic, moral. A Yogic Security Framework prioritizes **early intervention**, thereby **saving lives on both sides**, and **redirecting national wealth toward development, not destruction**.

Framing the Dilemma: Professions Built on Society's Problems

Some professions are designed to protect, defend, and heal society, but they are also inherently dependent on the presence of threats, suffering, or conflict. This creates a subtle contradiction: the more problems exist, the more these professions flourish — in recognition, compensation, and relevance. Yet, eliminating these roles altogether would make society vulnerable.

Profession	Problem it Exists to Solve	Contradiction
Doctor	Illness, injury, and poor health	Thrives when people are unwell; no illness = less work
Lawyer	Disputes, injustice, broken laws	Grows with conflict; fewer legal issues = lesser demand

Police	Crime, disorder, public safety	Depends on criminal acts to stay actively involved
Soldier / Defense	War, external threats, national security	Gains recognition through conflict; no war = minimal public attention or glory

Each profession carries a noble mission. However, their **daily activity and societal value often rise in proportion to human suffering, conflict, or danger**. This raises an uncomfortable but necessary question:

How do we sustain these professions ethically when their very existence is tied to problems we ideally want to eliminate?

Resolution Pathway: Evolve Their Purpose Toward Prevention, Peace, and Preparedness

Rather than eliminating these professions, the solution lies in **transforming their core roles** — from reactive responders to proactive peacekeepers, educators, and builders of systemic resilience.

Profession	Evolved Role / Purpose	How It Resolves the Dilemma
Doctor	Wellness guide, lifestyle mentor, public health educator	Focus shifts from treatment to prevention and lifelong vitality
Lawyer	Ethical advisor, mediator, law reformer	Promotes justice by preventing disputes and designing better systems
Police	Community builder, educator, youth mentor	Works to prevent crime through education, inclusion, and trust-building
Soldier / Defense	Strategic protector, peace ambassador, disaster responder	Maintains readiness, prevents war, supports peacekeeping and humanitarian missions

Key Insight

Professions of protection and healing must be incentivized not by crisis response, but by their role in preventing suffering and fostering harmony.

When society rewards **proactive efforts** — like health education, dispute avoidance, peaceful diplomacy, or community safety — rather than reactive success, these professions can thrive ethically.

Philosophical Note (Yogic / Dharmic View)

From a **Yogic and Vedantic perspective**, every role must align with *Dharma* — the cosmic order rooted in responsibility, harmony, and truth. A soldier who prevents war through deterrence, a doctor who keeps people healthy, a lawyer who helps prevent conflict, or a police officer who guides youth away from crime — these are **true karmic contributions**. In this view, **action without selfish desire (*nishkama karma*)** becomes the highest form of service.

Yogic Security vs. conventional Security

A Shift from Reaction to Conscious Response

Aspect	Retaliation-Based Security	Yogic Security Framework
Trigger Point	Post-attack or harm	Pre-emptive insight and awareness
Core Emotion	Fear, anger, revenge	Clarity, compassion, responsibility
Mindset	"Strike back to show power"	"Prevent harm through understanding and foresight"
Response Timing	After damage has occurred	Before threat manifests
Tools Used	Weapons, sanctions, aggression	Intelligence, AI prediction, diplomacy, inner training

Consequence	Escalation, casualties, resource loss	De-escalation, peacekeeping, minimal collateral impact
Role of Technology	Force multipliers, automation in attack/defense	Sensing, surveillance, peace prediction, energy mapping
Ethical Base	Retaliation justified by external harm	Action guided by *viveka* (discrimination) and *ahimsa*
Cost	High military, human, economic toll	Lower long-term costs; higher human development focus
Spiritual Alignment	Reactive, karmically heavy	Conscious, dharmic, lightening karmic load
End Result	Temporary dominance, fear cycles	Sustainable peace, trust, and balance

Solution Approach

1. Air Quality as Agenda #1: Without Pure Air, Yoga Fails

If the air is polluted, Pranayama doesn't work—and when Pranayama fails, Yoga fails. Therefore, air quality is not a secondary concern but a foundational pillar of individual and societal security.

Organizations, schools, and institutions must:

- Install real-time AQI monitors in all workspaces and public buildings.
- Publicly display AQI data and incorporate it into institutional reporting.
- Make "Air Quality Review" a mandatory agenda item in every meeting across all sectors.

- Design clean air zones with natural ventilation, green spaces, and zero-toxin policies.
- Ban or restrict wellness, yoga, or meditation programs in spaces that don't meet minimum air quality standards.

This is non-negotiable. Yoga cannot be implemented successfully without a breathable environment. Before practicing breathwork, we must ensure the breath is worth working with.

2. Yoga as the Superset Department: Structural Autonomy & Governance

Yoga must be recognized not as a sport or health program but as a governing framework for national and organizational well-being. A separate and autonomous department or ministry—like the "Ministry of Yogic Sciences"—should be established with authority across education, healthcare, corporate compliance, and environmental affairs.

Every national policy or institutional decision should be aligned with yogic values. Yoga-certified advisors and auditors should have mandatory seats on regulatory and strategic boards.

3. Curriculum Reform: Mandating Yogic Science Education

Yogic Science must be introduced as a core academic subject from the foundational years of education, alongside Maths, Science, and Social Studies.

Core components should include:

- Asanas and Pranayama
- Emotional intelligence and self-discipline
- Yogic diet and lifestyle
- Ayurveda and holistic health principles
- Environmental and ethical consciousness (Ahimsa, Satya, Aparigraha)

Schools must include both theoretical understanding and daily practice. This is an investment in a generation of mentally resilient, physically fit, and environmentally conscious citizens.

4. Corporate and Institutional Mandate: Health-First Operations

Organizations must adopt a Health-First operational philosophy:

- Implement the Follow-the-Sun model to align with natural human rhythms and reduce burnout.
- Assess every job role for its physical and mental impact. Redesign or discontinue roles that degrade health.
- Introduce quarterly "Yogic Health Audits" for employee well-being, air quality, food safety, and wellness program effectiveness.
- Incorporate Yoga-based stress prevention strategies into HR, performance management, and team development.

5. Redefining Security: From Outer Armor to Inner Alignment

Security must be understood as an internal state of stability and clarity, not just as an external control mechanism.

We must move from a society based on pathogenesis (responding to disease) to one rooted in salutogenesis (generating health). Stress-free citizens create safer environments. A weak population—physically or mentally—leads to weak systems, poor productivity, and greater vulnerability to crises.

This book invites readers to rediscover Yogic science as a powerful and practical path to inner stability. In a world increasingly dependent on external tools for protection, it is inner alignment that offers the most lasting security.

Consider a common scene: as the school day ends, children often burst out of classrooms with overwhelming excitement—shouting, running, even engaging in risky behavior like hanging out of bus windows. Such exuberance, while natural, can lead to danger. Traditional disciplinary methods, especially those rooted in fear, rarely bring lasting change.

Yogic techniques such as Instant Relaxation Technique (IRT), Quick Relaxation Technique (QRT), or Deep Relaxation Technique (DRT) offer a gentle yet effective solution. Just 5–10 minutes of guided stillness at the end of the school day can help activate the parasympathetic nervous system, calming the mind and body before transition.

This principle extends well beyond classrooms. High-stakes professions—pilots, doctors, emergency responders—can benefit immensely from brief relaxation practices before and after duty. Even moviegoers, especially after viewing intense or violent content, could transition more peacefully into busy public spaces if a short period of relaxation was introduced before exiting the theatre.

Organizations, too, must evolve. People managers and leaders should be trained in Yoga to cultivate mental clarity, emotional regulation, and conscious decision-making. When leaders are centered, their teams thrive.

What may seem novel today could soon be a necessity. Inner peace is no longer a luxury—it is the foundation of true, stress-free security.

6. Quality and Health Functions: From Back-End to Frontline

Functions like Food Safety, Quality Control, and Environmental Inspection must be elevated from support roles to decision-making authorities.

Every product, service, or policy must undergo a Health and Yogic Impact Assessment (HYIA). No project should move forward without approval from the quality and health control departments.

New metrics should include:

- Pranic integrity
- Environmental sustainability
- Psychological wellness outcomes
- Post-use impact on human and ecological health

7. Governance Shift: CEOs Must Report to Health and Environmental Officers

It's time for a paradigm shift in organizational governance. Institutions must not just measure success in revenue, but in how safe, sustainable, and life-affirming they are for future generations.

CEOs and top decision-makers must ask themselves one transformative question:

"Would I proudly refer my own children or grandchildren to work in this company?"

If the answer is no, then that organization is not truly secure—regardless of profits, policies, or perks.

Similarly, food production units must ask:

"Would I feed this product to my own child every day without hesitation?"

If not, then the food is not safe for the public either.

Manufacturers of plastic toys, gadgets, or consumer goods should ask:

"Would I allow my own child to use or play with this product for hours?"

Educational institutions must reflect:

"Is this curriculum and environment something I would want for my own children?"

Corporate leaders must apply this personalized ethical lens to every decision they make—because real leadership begins when personal accountability meets public impact.

Additionally:

- CEOs should co-report to Chief Health, Environmental, or Yogic Governance Officers to ensure that financial leadership is balanced with human and ecological stewardship.
- KPIs must include long-term human impact, environmental health scores, and employee well-being—not just quarterly numbers.

This isn't just governance reform. It's a cultural awakening.

Until leadership decisions are guided by empathy, legacy thinking, and long-term vitality, no system can be truly secure.

8. Organic and Life-Centric Economy: Real Profits Come from Health

Promote and reward:

- Organic and natural product industries
- Toxin-free, zero-waste manufacturing
- Holistic service ecosystems (Yoga, Ayurveda, traditional medicine, natural healing)

Offer government and corporate incentives for businesses that protect health, restore soil and air quality, and reduce dependency on pharmaceuticals or synthetic interventions. A healthy citizenry is the most valuable national asset.

9. Cultural Shift to Salutogenesis

Encourage every citizen, leader, and institution to consistently ask:

"Is this job, activity, school, policy, or product strengthening human health or weakening it?"

Let this single question govern all decisions. By embedding this mindset at every level—from family to federal—we transition from survival mode to sustainable thriving.

If any of these actions seem difficult to implement or hard to justify, then focus on this single-agenda manifesto presented as an algorithm

The Algorithm to Build a Healthy Society: Begin with Pancha Bhootha Protection

Before we chase technological advancement, GDP growth, or political dominance, we must remember one fundamental **truth**:

We are not outside the environment—we are inside it.

Just like fish live in water, we live in the reverberating chamber of nature. Our thoughts, words, actions—everything we emit—echoes through the Pancha Bhootha and returns to us as either harmony or havoc.

If we protect and purify these five elemental forces, there will be no need for complex political manifestos or public campaigns. Nature itself will become the guardian of our health, economy, and peace.

1. Air (Vayu): Breath is the Currency of Life

Air is the very first life-giver. It doesn't just fill our lungs—it fuels our brain, balances our emotions, and powers our prana (life force).

- Any industrial project or innovation that pollutes the air must be automatically rejected—no exceptions, no compromises.
- Governments and businesses must encourage nature-aligned innovation—technologies that clean, not contaminate.
- Pranayama fails when the air is toxic. And when Pranayama fails, Yoga fails. Life fails.

Clean air is not a right—it is a responsibility shared by all.

2. Water (Jala): The Body's Sacred River

Water is not just H_2O. It is memory, vibration, energy, and emotion. Our bodies are nearly 70% water. Polluted water means polluted minds, weakened bodies, and disturbed emotions.

- Every policy, project, or product must pass a "Water Impact Test."
- No factory, process, or chemical should be allowed if it contaminates rivers, lakes, or groundwater—even minimally.
- Encourage innovations that revive water bodies, recharge aquifers, and treat water as sacred, not as a commodity.

When you poison water, you poison the next generation.

3. Fire (Agni): The Fire Within and Without

Fire governs digestion, vision, intellect, metabolism, and transformation. The quality of the fire element impacts both internal health and external sustainability.

- Ban technologies and industries that create destructive or unnatural heat, emissions, and toxic combustion.

- Promote cooking, lighting, and energy systems that respect Agni—clean-burning fuels, solar energy, and natural light.
- Fire must be sacred, not suffocating. Let it illuminate and transform, not incinerate.

When fire is respected, it heals. When it's abused, it destroys.

4. Earth (Prithvi): Our Foundation, Our Food

Earth is the body beneath our feet—and the food in our plate. It gives shape to everything. It nourishes plants, animals, and us.

- Agricultural policies must prioritize soil health, organic farming, and biodiversity.
- Mining, construction, and real estate projects must pass strict ecological integrity tests.
- Fertile land must never be sacrificed for short-term industrial gain.

A nation with dead soil cannot raise a living society.

5. Space (Akasha): The Silent Witness

Space is not emptiness. It holds sound, vibration, memory, and consciousness. The way we speak, think, and use digital or physical space affects our mental and spiritual well-being.

- Noise pollution, digital toxicity, and cluttered environments must be treated as serious mental pollutants.
- Encourage architecture, media, education, and urban planning that promote silence, clarity, and inner spaciousness.
- Sacred spaces—temples, forests, meditative zones—must be preserved and expanded.

If Space is corrupted, clarity disappears. Confusion and chaos become the new normal.

Final Insight:

If the Pancha Bhootha are cared for,

- Our breath becomes medicine.
- Our food becomes nutrition.
- Our water becomes nectar.
- Our thoughts become sacred.
- Our society becomes secure.

So here's the truth every leader, policymaker, and citizen must remember:

"Protecting the Pancha Bhootha is not a spiritual luxury—it is the only scientific, economic, and political strategy that guarantees a secure future."

Let this be the new-age algorithm for peace, prosperity, and stress-free security.

Policy-making is one of the most sacred responsibilities in any nation—far more critical than performing a surgery, piloting an aircraft, or even standing on the frontlines as a soldier.

Why? Because a single policy has the power to uplift or destroy an entire generation. The environment we live in—social, economic, educational, ecological—is profoundly shaped by the decisions of policymakers.

When policies are crafted with short-sightedness or selfish intent, they don't just fail systems—they fracture lives. Therefore, policy-making must be treated with the highest level of consciousness, integrity, and accountability

If there is one place where true and lasting change must begin, it is in the realm of policy making. And policy makers are not limited to government officials—they are all around us. They are school principals, founders, CEOs, HR leaders, ministers, heads of institutions, and even the heads of families—a mother, a father, or anyone who influences the environment in which others grow and live.

To every policy maker in every walk of life, I offer this heartfelt appeal: You hold a sacred opportunity to transform the spaces you lead into divine environments—where human life, from birth to death, can be lived with peace, health, dignity, and purpose. Let your decisions become the foundation for conscious living and collective well-being.

The path to a stress-free, secure, and harmonious society begins with you. Whether you lead a home, a school, a company, or a country—you have the power to turn this earth into heaven.

A Yogic Reframing of Security:

Retaliation is the response of a reactive mind.

Prevention is the action of a still, aware consciousness.

The highest security intelligence is not force—it is foresight.

"True power lies not in punishing the enemy, but in preventing the enmity from arising."

— Inspired by the Yogic Vision of Dharma-Based Security